OVER
AND UNDER

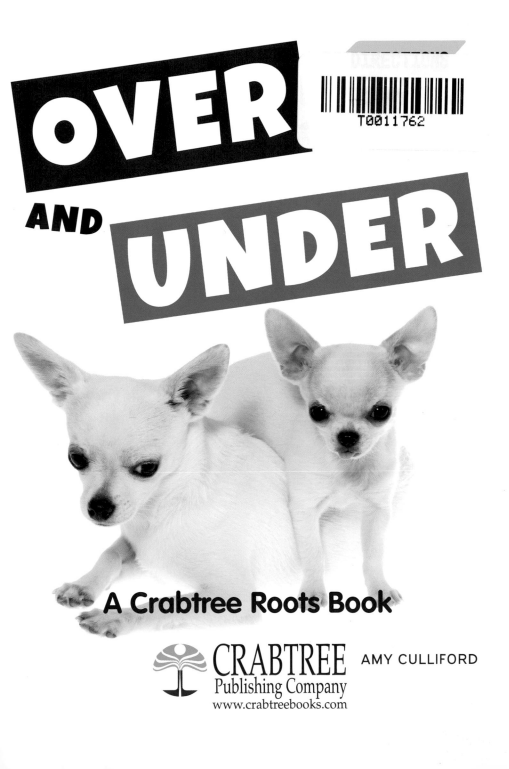

A Crabtree Roots Book

CRABTREE
Publishing Company
www.crabtreebooks.com

AMY CULLIFORD

School-to-Home Support for Caregivers and Teachers

This book helps children grow by letting them practice reading. Here are a few guiding questions to help the reader with building his or her comprehension skills. Possible answers appear here in red.

Before Reading:

• What do I think this book is about?
  • *I think this book is about directions.*
  • *I think this book is about what over and under mean.*

• What do I want to learn about this topic?
  • *I want to learn what it looks like when something is over and when something is under.*
  • *I want to learn what it means when an object is over another object.*

During Reading:

• I wonder why...
  • *I wonder why the bridge has cables.*
  • *I wonder why people sit under trees.*

• What have I learned so far?
  • *I have learned that a ball can be over or under a net.*
  • *I have learned what over and under directions look like.*

After Reading:

• What details did I learn about this topic?
  • *I have learned that people can swim under water and drive on a bridge over water.*
  • *I have learned that things that are over other things are usually higher off the ground.*

• Read the book again and look for the vocabulary words.
  • *I see the word **net** on page 3 and the word **trees** on page 7. The other vocabulary word is found on page 14.*

This ball is over
the **net**.

This ball is under the net.

A bird flies over the **trees**.

People sit under
the tree.

The **bridge** is over the water.

Terry is under
the water.

Word List

Sight Words

ball	over	this
bird	people	under
flies	sit	water
is	the	

Words to Know

bridge

net

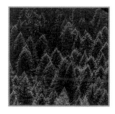

trees

34 Words

This ball is over the **net**.

This ball is under the net.

A bird flies over the **trees**.

People sit under the tree.

The **bridge** is over the water.

Terry is under the water.

DIRECTIONS IN MY World

OVER AND UNDER

Written by: Amy Culliford

Designed by: Rhea Wallace

Series Development: James Earley

Proofreader: Janine Deschenes

Educational Consultant: Marie Lemke M.Ed.

Photographs:
Shutterstock: StudioPetPhotos: cover, p. 1; zieusin: p. 3, 14; Kobkob: p. 5; muratart: p. 6, 14; Jim Lambert: p. 9; ESBProfessional: p. 10, 11, 14; Andrey Armyagov: p. 13

Library and Archives Canada Cataloguing in Publication

CIP available at Library and Archives Canada

Library of Congress Cataloging-in-Publication Data

CIP available at Library of Congress

Crabtree Publishing Company

www.crabtreebooks.com   1-800-387-7650

Published in the United States
Crabtree Publishing
347 Fifth Avenue, Suite 1402-145
New York, NY, 10016

Published in Canada
Crabtree Publishing
616 Welland Ave.
St. Catharines, Ontario L2M 5V6